$\mathcal{A}$DVENT *and* $\mathcal{C}$HRISTMAS $\mathcal{W}$ISDOM

—— *from* ——

$\mathcal{S}$t. $\mathcal{A}$ugustine

ADVENT and CHRISTMAS WISDOM

from

St. Augustine

Agnes Cunningham, SSCM

Liguori

LIGUORI, MISSOURI

Imprimi Potest:
Harry Grile, CSsR, Provincial
Denver Province, The Redemptorists

Published by Liguori Publications, Liguori, Missouri 63057

To order, call 800-325-9521, or visit liguori.org

Library of Congress Cataloging-in-Publication Data
Cunningham, Agnes, 1923-
 Advent and Christmas wisdom from St. Augustine / Agnes Cunningham, SSCM.—
First Edition.
 pages cm
1. Augustine, Saint, Bishop of Hippo. 2. Advent. 3. Christmas. I. Title.
 BR65.A9C86 2013
 242'.33—dc23
 2013018517
p ISBN: 978-0-7648-2030-4
e ISBN: 978-0-7648-6861-0

The texts from St. Augustine that comprise the "Wisdom" sections of this book were gathered by and are the responsibility of the author, who obtained them from books listed on page 105.

Compliant with *The Roman Missal*, third edition.

The English translation of the Canticle of Simeon is by the International Consultation on English Texts.

Liguori Publications, a nonprofit corporation, is an apostolate of The Redemptorists. To learn more about The Redemptorists, visit Redemptorists.com.

Printed in the United States of America
17 16 15 14 13 / 5 4 3 2 1
First Edition

Contents

Introduction

Who is St. Augustine? Why do we look to him as a guide in our search for wisdom through the season of Advent?

This saint, recognized among the Church doctors as the Doctor of Grace and the Doctor of Doctors, was born on November 13, 354, in Tagaste, Numidia, to a devout Christian woman, Monica, and a pagan father, Patricius, who became a Christian shortly before his death. Augustine was one of three children, along with a brother, Navigius, and a sister whose name we do not know, the abbess of a monastery in Hippo.

Augustine has been called the "theologian's theologian." However, it is not because of his outstanding works in theology and philosophy that we look to him as a wisdom figure. In his search for truth, Augustine's keen intellect first led him away from Christianity until he saw the errors of the heretical sects he had followed. The wisdom to which Augustine introduces us, founded on and nourished by his gifts of nature and grace, has its roots in the story of his conversion through the abundant redemption that transformed his life into a confession of praise.

Under the guidance and instructions of St. Ambrose, Augustine was baptized with his friend, Alypius, and his son, Adeodatus, at the age of 33. He retired with a group of friends to live a monastic life until he was called to the priesthood. He continued to live an ascetical life, a life of prayer and contemplation.

As he continued his studies in theology, Augustine discovered and probed the richness of the Catholic faith in Christ, the wisdom of God. Through Christ, he discovered, he was captivated by and embraced God, who is "beauty, ever ancient, ever new." Consecrated a bishop in the year 395 or 396, he cared for his diocese as well as the Church in Africa and, indeed, the universal Catholic Church. As a dedicated pastor of souls, he learned to draw from the deep riches of his own spiritual life to become a sure guide for his people. His legacy has been an inspiration throughout the ages, and we know we can trust him as we begin our journey along the way of wisdom into the mystery of the Incarnation.

How to Use This Book

Advent—that period of great anticipatory joy—is a time of preparation for the celebration of Christ's arrival in Bethlehem as a helpless infant. In the Western liturgy, Advent begins four Sundays before December 25—the Sunday closest to November 30, which is the feast of St. Andrew, one of Jesus' first disciples.

The annual commemoration of Christ's birth begins the Christmas cycle of the liturgical year—a cycle that runs from Christmas Day to the baptism of the Lord. In keeping with the unfolding of the message of the liturgical year, this book is designed to be used from the first Sunday of Advent through twelve days of the Christmas cycle, or until January 6.

The four weeks of Advent are often thought of as symbolizing the four ways Christ comes into the world: (1) his birth as a helpless infant; (2) his arrival in the hearts of believers; (3) his death; and (4) his arrival on Judgment Day.

Because Christmas falls on a different day of the week each year, the fourth week of Advent seldom lasts a full week—it is abruptly, joyously, and solemnly abrogated by the annual coming of Christ at Christmas. Christ's Second Coming will also one day abruptly interrupt our sojourn here on earth.

In this book, each day's passages begin with the words of St. Augustine. Next is a related excerpt from Scripture that is followed by a prayer built on the ideas from the two preceding passages.

Finally, an Advent or Christmas action suggests ways to apply the messages to daily life.

Because the length of Advent varies, this book includes material for twenty-eight days. These daily readings make up **Part I**. You can skip the "extra" entries, or you can fit them all in by doubling up.

Part II begins with Christmas Day and contains materials for twelve days of the Christmas season.

Part III proposes two optional formats for using each day as part of a longer liturgical observance similar to Night Prayer, combined with a version of the Office of Readings. The purpose of these readings is to enrich the Advent/Christmas/Epiphany season of the liturgical year and set up a means by which individuals, families, or groups can observe the true meaning of the season.

PART I

~

READINGS *for* ADVENT

DAY 1

WISDOM

You, Lord my God, are the giver of life and a body to a baby. As we see, you have endowed it with senses. You have coordinated the limbs. You have adorned it with a beautiful form, and for the coherence and preservation of the whole you have implanted all the instincts of a living being. You therefore command me to praise you..."and to sing to your name, Most High" Psalm 91:2. No one else could do that except you, the one from whom every kind of being is derived. The supreme beauty, you give distinct form to all things and by your law impose order on everything.

CONFESSIONS, I, VII

SCRIPTURE

LORD, you have probed me, you know me; you know when I sit and stand; you understand my thoughts from afar. My travels and my rest you mark; with all my ways you are familiar. Even before a word is on my tongue, LORD, you know it all. Behind and before you encircle me and rest your hand upon me. You formed my inmost being; you knit me in my mother's womb. I praise you, because I am wonderfully made; wonderful are your works! My very self you know. My bones are not hidden from you, when I was being made in secret, fashioned in the depths of the earth.

PSALM 139:1–5, 13–15

PRAYER

Loving Creator, in the Incarnation of your eternal word you have revealed the mystery of your divine fatherhood and your adoption of us as your daughters and sons. Through Christ and with Christ, in the power of your Spirit, may we be faithful to your call and give glory to your name during the days of this blessed season. Amen.

ADVENT ACTION

Take time today, in gratitude for the gift of life and the grace of life in Christ, to pray for your parents and for the priest who baptized you.

✓ DAY 2

WISDOM

By nature we are not God; by nature we are men; by sin we are not just. So God became a just man to intercede with God for sinful man. The sinner did not match the just, but man did match man. So he applied to us the similarity of his humanity to take away the dissimilarity of our iniquity, and becoming a partaker of our mortality he made us partakers of his divinity. It was surely right that the death of the sinner issuing from the stern necessity of condemnation should be undone by the death of the just man issuing from the voluntary freedom of mercy....

THE TRINITY, IV, 4

SCRIPTURE

Who would believe what we have heard?...He had no majestic bearing to catch our eye, no beauty to draw us to him. He was spurned and avoided by men, a man of suffering, knowing pain....Yet it was our pain that he bore, our sufferings he endured....[H]e was pierced for our sins, crushed for our iniquity. He bore the punishment that makes us whole, by his wounds we were healed. We had all gone astray like sheep, all following our own way; but the LORD laid upon him the guilt of us all....Because of his anguish...my servant shall justify the many, their iniquity he shall bear....[H]e surrendered himself to death, was counted among the transgressors, bore the sins of many, and interceded for the transgressors.

ISAIAH 53:1–6, 11–12

PRAYER

Merciful God, love for your eternal Son did not prevent you from asking him to carry the weight of our sins and restore the plan you had for our happiness. Your Son's love for you led him to accept your will completely. We have been blessed with graces beyond anything we could have imagined. Freed from guilt and shame, we rejoice in the life to which we are now called to share as your faithful daughters and sons with and in Christ. Amen.

ADVENT ACTION

Accept the most difficult thing you encounter today as a prayer of intercession for someone you know who has rejected God from his or her life.

DAY 3

✓ WISDOM

Before I existed you were, and I had no being to which you could grant existence. Nevertheless here I am as a result of your goodness, which goes before all that you made me to be and all out of which you made me. You had no need of me. I do not possess such goodness as to give you help....It is not as if I could so serve you as to prevent you becoming weary in your work, or that your power is diminished if it lacks my homage....To you I owe my being and the goodness of my being.

CONFESSIONS, XIII, 1

SCRIPTURE

Bless the LORD, my soul; all my being, bless his holy name! Bless the LORD, my soul; and do not forget all his gifts, Who pardons all your sins, and heals all your ills, Who redeems your life from the pit, and crowns you with mercy and compassion, Who fills your days with good things, so your youth is renewed like the eagle's....For as the heavens tower over the earth, so his mercy towers over those who fear him. As far as the east is from the west, so far has he removed our sins from us. As a father has compassion on his children, so the LORD has compassion on those who fear him. For he knows how we are formed, remembers that we are dust.

PSALM 103:1–5, 11–14

PRAYER

Wonderful God, how can I ever thank you for the gifts you have bestowed on me? I count the blessings that have marked my life from its beginnings. Even the challenges and sorrows of the past have led me to understand more clearly your goodness and the purpose for which you created me. Guide me through your Holy Spirit along the pathway that still lies ahead until I reach the end to which you continually call me. Amen.

ADVENT ACTION

Live this day in the joy of the knowledge that God carries you in his love and wills only what is best for you, no matter what difficulties you have to bear at this time in your life.

DAY 4

WISDOM

In this Beginning, God, you made heaven and earth, in your Word, in your Son, in your power, in your wisdom, in your truth speaking in a wonderful way and making in a wonderful way. Who can comprehend it? Who will give an account of it in words? What is the light which shines right through me and strikes my heart without hurting? It fills me with terror and burning love ....Wisdom, wisdom it is which shines right through me, cutting a path through the cloudiness which returns to cover me as I fall away under the darkness and the load of my punishments.

CONFESSIONS, XI, IX

SCRIPTURE

The Lord created human beings from the earth, and makes them return to earth again. A limited number of days he gave them, but granted them authority over everything on earth. He endowed them with strength like his own, and made them in his image. He put fear of them in all flesh, and gave them dominion over beasts and birds. Discernment, tongues, and eyes, ears, and a mind for thinking he gave them. With knowledge and understanding he filled them; good and evil he showed them. He put fear of him into their hearts to show them the grandeur of his works, that they might describe the wonders of his deeds and praise his holy name....All their works are clear as the sun to him, and his eyes are ever upon their ways....Later he will rise up and repay them....

SIRACH 17:1–10, 19, 23

PRAYER

Creating God, you never cease to sustain me with the breath of life. You have given me a mind to seek and know you, a heart to love and cherish you. You are ever mindful of who I am and what I need. Let me not be overwhelmed by the burdens of life that threaten to make me doubt your love. Do not let me forget your greatest gift, Jesus, your Son, in whom the fullness of your presence is ever mine. Amen.

ADVENT ACTION

Today share with someone you know the way in which God is working in your life at this time, the assurance you have of his love for you, and the ways you seek to be grateful to him.

DAY 5

WISDOM

Late have I loved you, beauty so old and so new: late have I loved you. And see, you were within and I was in the external world and sought you there....You were with me, and I was not with you.... You called and cried out loud and shattered my deafness. You were radiant and resplendent, you put to flight my blindness. You were fragrant and I drew in my breath and now pant after you. I tasted you, and feel but hunger and thirst for you. You touched me, and I am set on fire to attain the peace which is yours.

CONFESSIONS, X, VII

SCRIPTURE

I love you, LORD, my strength, LORD, my rock, my fortress, my deliverer, my God, my rock of refuge, my shield, my saving horn, my stronghold! Praised be the LORD, I exclaim! I have been delivered from my enemies....He reached down from on high and seized me; drew me out of the deep waters. He rescued me from my mighty enemy, from foes too powerful for me.... He set me free in the open; he rescued me because he loves me.

PSALM 18:2–4, 17–18, 20

PRAYER

Dear God, if there is anything I know about you, it is that you are love. You never cease to surround us with love—love that is eternal, gentle, faithful, and true. You ask only that we love you in return. Because this is beyond the limits of our human hearts, you have given us your beloved Son to love you for us. With Christ, I can say that I love you. Let me sing it with my whole being! Amen.

ADVENT ACTION

Ask God today to let you see how you fail to love someone with whom you are in daily contact. Ask for the grace to learn to love that person.

DAY 6

WISDOM

He who for us is life itself descended here and endured our death and slew it by the abundance of his life....First he came into the Virgin's womb where the human creation was married to him, so that mortal flesh should not for ever be mortal....He did not delay, but ran crying out loud by his words, deeds, death, life, descent, and ascent—calling us to return to him. And he has gone from our sight that we should "return to our heart" (Isaiah 46:8) and find him there. He went away and behold, here he is.

CONFESSIONS, IV, XII

SCRIPTURE

A voice proclaims: In the wilderness prepare the way of the LORD! Make straight in the wasteland a highway for our God! Every valley shall be lifted up, every mountain and hill made low; the rugged land shall be a plain, the rough country a broad valley. Then the glory of the LORD shall be revealed, and all flesh shall see it together; for the mouth of the LORD has spoken....Go up onto a high mountain, Zion, herald of good news! Cry out at the top of your voice, Jerusalem, herald of good news! Cry out, do not fear! Say to the cities of Judah: Here is your God! Here comes with power the LORD God, who rules by his strong arm; Here is his reward with him, his recompense before him.

ISAIAH 40:3–5, 9–11

PRAYER

Gentle and loving God, your Word broke into our world with its unholy noise and clamor, but eternal silence thundered above every distracting, seductive voice to call us to awareness of the gifted promise that is ours. We eagerly seek to turn our hearts and our steps into the pathways of peace and reconciliation, away from all that would stand in the way of our ascent with Christ along the highway that leads to you. Be with us on this Advent journey. Amen.

ADVENT ACTION

Pray today for the gift of a discerning spirit so the ears of your heart may recognize the voice of the silent Word in Mary's womb and respond to God's call as his divine will is revealed to you.

✓ **DAY 7**

WISDOM

Before He was made, He was; and His was the power, because He was all-powerful, to be made and to remain what He was. Abiding with His Father, He made for Himself a mother; and when He was made in the womb of His mother, He remained in the heart of His Father.... [T]he Word did not become flesh by ceasing to be; on the contrary, the flesh, lest it should cease to be, was joined to the Word, so that, just as man is body and soul, Christ might be God and man, not in a confusion of nature, but in the unity of a person.

CHRISTMAS 4

SCRIPTURE

[W]hen the fullness of time had come, God sent his Son, born of a woman, born under the law, to ransom those under the law, so that we might receive adoption. As proof that you are children, God sent the spirit of his Son into our hearts, crying out, "Abba, Father!" So you are no longer a slave but a child, and if a child then also an heir, through God.

GALATIANS 4:4–7

PRAYER

Gracious Father, it was not enough for you to send your Son into our world to redeem us. We know that, when we look on the face of the Son of Mary, we see you. In Jesus, your Son, we are your adopted children, chosen to share in the riches of your love and called to rejoice with you in the New Jerusalem where we shall praise you with all the holy ones for all eternity. Grant us so to live that, when you look upon us, you see your beloved Son incarnate in us through the power of your Spirit. Amen.

ADVENT ACTION

Make an effort today to look on everyone you meet, especially anyone who is unpleasant, as a person chosen by the Father of Jesus to share the gift of adoption, with you, in Christ.

DAY 8

WISDOM

My brethren, what miracles! What prodigies! The laws of nature are changed in the case of man. God is born. A virgin becomes pregnant with man. The Word of God marries the woman who knows no man. She is now at the same time both mother and virgin. She becomes a mother, yet she remains a virgin. The virgin bears a son yet she does not know man; she remains untouched, yet she is not barren. He alone was born without sin, for she bore him without the embrace of a man, not by the concupiscence of the flesh but by the obedience of the mind.

SERMO 13 DE TEMPORE

SCRIPTURE

Who has measured with his palm the waters, marked off the heavens with a span, held in his fingers the dust of the earth, weighed the mountains in scales and the hills in a balance? Who has directed the spirit of the LORD, or instructed him as his counselor? Whom did he consult to gain knowledge? Who taught him the path of judgment, or showed him the way of understanding?...To whom can you liken God?...Do you not know? Have you not heard? The LORD is God from of old, creator of the ends of the earth....They that hope in the LORD will renew their strength, they will soar on eagles' wings; They will run and not grow weary, walk and not grow faint.

ISAIAH 40:12–14, 18, 28, 31

PRAYER

Wondrous God, all that you have created overwhelms us with its grandeur and splendor beyond anything we can begin to imagine! You have gifted us with insight and the ability to continue to unfold the hidden treasures of your creation. And yet all that we see and know fades before this amazing, unheard of reality: the Incarnation of your beloved Son and the grace and beauty of the woman chosen to be his Mother. May I grow in thanksgiving for this extraordinary gift. Amen.

ADVENT ACTION

Cherish the grace of the liturgical season in which the Church invites you to enter into the mystery of the Incarnation through some sign of your love for Jesus and Mary that you are able to offer God today.

DAY 9

WISDOM

The Truth which abides in the bosom of the Father, is sprung out of the earth to dwell also in the bosom of a mother. The Truth which contains the world, is sprung out of the earth to be borne in the hands of a woman. The Truth which is the food of incorruption for the angels, is sprung out of the earth to receive milk from the breasts of woman. The Truth which the heavens cannot contain, is sprung out of the earth to be placed in a manger!...Wake up, O man—it was for you that God was made man!

SERMONS FOR CHRISTMAS 3

SCRIPTURE

Who may go up the mountain of the LORD? Who can stand in his holy place? "The clean of hand and pure of heart, who has not given his soul to useless things, what is vain. He will receive blessings from the LORD, and justice from his saving God. Such is the generation that seeks him, that seeks the face of the God of Jacob." Lift up your heads, O gates; be lifted, you ancient portals, that the king of glory may enter. Who is this king of glory? The LORD, strong and mighty, the LORD, mighty in war. Lift up your heads, O gates; rise up, you ancient portals, that the king of glory may enter. Who is this king of glory? The LORD of hosts, he is the king of glory.

PSALM 24:3–10

PRAYER

Great God! You knock at the doors of our hearts calling us to contemplate the mystery of a God-made-man, the wonder of a woman chosen to be the Mother of God! How can we take one step toward the goal of all our Advent seeking and waiting? Help us to persevere in the assurance that Jesus and Mary are with us to lead us out of darkness into light, out of error into the blessed grace of your faithful love and care. Amen.

ADVENT ACTION

Take a quiet moment today to offer the Hail Mary in the spirit of the Archangel Gabriel who first brought to Mary the announcement of the choice God had made of her to bring about the wonder of the Incarnation.

DAY 10

WISDOM

[B]ecause God's promises seemed impossible to men—equality with the angels in exchange for mortality, corruption, poverty, weakness, dust and ashes—God not only make a written contract with men to win their belief but also established a mediator of his good faith, not a prince or angel or archangel, but his only Son. He wanted, through his Son, to show us and give us the way he would lead us to the goal he had promised.

It was not enough for God to make his Son our guide to the way; he made him the way itself, that you might travel with him as leader, and by him as the way.

ON PSALM 109

SCRIPTURE

He is the image of the invisible God, the firstborn of all creation. For in him were created all things in heaven and on earth, the visible and the invisible, whether thrones or dominions or principalities or powers; all things were created through him and for him. He is before all things, and in him all things hold together. He is the head of the body, the church. He is the beginning, the firstborn from the dead, that in all things he himself might be preeminent. For in him all the fullness was pleased to dwell, and through him to reconcile all things for him, making peace by the blood of his cross.

COLOSSIANS 1:15–20

PRAYER

Loving Father, as the Church leads us through this holy season toward the celebration of the coming of Christ, we thank you for the gift of this precious Son whose presence in our lives is the assurance that we shall, indeed, have the grace to continue the time of waiting during the coming weeks. We know, too, that Christ's coming is the sign that the road ahead, beyond Advent and Christmas, will take us in faith and hope toward the goal to which you call us: eternal life in our true home with you. Amen.

ADVENT ACTION

Find someone today with whom you can share the meaning of Christ's presence in your life and your deep gratitude to God for the gift of his beloved Son with whom you can cry, "Abba, Father!"

DAY 11

WISDOM

What man knows all the treasures of wisdom and knowledge hidden in Christ...? Scripture says: *Although he was rich he became poor for our sake to enrich us by his poverty.* He showed himself poor when he assumed our mortal nature and destroyed death, yet he promised us riches, for he had not been robbed of his wealth but was keeping it in reserve....The only Son of God became a son of man to make many men sons of God. He instructed slaves by showing himself in the form of a slave, and now he enables free men to see him in the form of God.

SERMON 194

SCRIPTURE

[S]ince in the wisdom of God the world did not come to know God through wisdom, it was the will of God through the foolishness of the proclamation to save those who have faith. For Jews demand signs and Greeks look for wisdom, but we proclaim Christ crucified, a stumbling block to Jews and foolishness to Gentiles, but to those who are called, Jews and Greeks alike, Christ the power of God and the wisdom of God. For the foolishness of God is wiser than human wisdom, and the weakness of God is stronger than human strength.

1 CORINTHIANS 1:21–25

PRAYER

All-knowing God, you desire that all persons on earth reach the fullness of the humanity you have given us through knowing you and Jesus Christ whom you have sent. For this purpose, you have placed within us an unquenchable desire for truth and love. Until we realize that you, great God, are truth that has no measure and love that has no bounds, we search in vain, misled by error and self-seeking. Be light in our lives and do not cease to probe and pursue us until we belong entirely to you. Amen.

ADVENT ACTION

Try in a special way today to witness to the truth in a situation that you recognize as a threat to the integrity of a person whose reputation may be at stake.

✓ DAY 12

WISDOM

The true Mediator you showed to humanity in your secret mercy. You sent him so that from his example they should learn humility....He appeared among mortal sinners as the immortal righteous one, mortal like humanity, righteous like God. Because the wages of righteousness are life and peace (Romans 6:23), being united with God by his righteousness he made void the death of justified sinners, a death which it was his will to share in common with them....

How you have loved us, good Father: You did not "spare your only Son but delivered him up for us sinners" (Romans 8:32).

CONFESSIONS, X, XLIII

SCRIPTURE

For when peaceful stillness encompassed everything and the night in its swift course was half spent, Your all-powerful word from heaven's royal throne leapt into the doomed land, a fierce warrior bearing the sharp sword of your inexorable decree.... Yet not for long did the anger last. For the blameless man hastened to be their champion, bearing the weapon of his special office, prayer and the propitiation of incense; He withstood the wrath and put a stop to the calamity, showing that he was your servant....For on his full-length robe was the whole world, and ancestral glories were carved on the four rows of stones, and your grandeur was on the crown upon his head.

WISDOM 18:14–16, 21, 24

PRAYER

Holy God, we know that Advent is meant to prepare us for the final coming of your beloved Son when he returns at the end of time in majesty and glory. We do not want to be overcome by unholy fear and dread. Help us to remember that the Lord of glory is the unborn Child in Mary's womb whom we shall adore as the divine Child in the crib. May his gentle touch even now inspire us to live in faith and love. Amen.

ADVENT ACTION

Take time today to reflect on the three comings of Christ: in time past, in the graces of the present, in the challenge of the future. What do they say to you?

DAY 13

WISDOM

If Adam had not fallen from you, there would not have flowed from his loins that salty sea-water the human race—deeply inquisitive, like a sea in a stormy swell, restlessly unstable. Then there would have been no need for your ministers at work in many waters to resort to mystic actions and words in the realm of the bodily senses....[F]or human beings after instruction, initiation, and subjection to corporeal sacraments do not make further progress unless in the spiritual realm their soul comes to live on another level and subsequent to the words of initiation, looks towards their perfection (Hebrews 6:1).

CONFESSIONS, XIII, XX

SCRIPTURE

Live by the Spirit and you will certainly not gratify the desire of the flesh. For the flesh has desires against the Spirit, and the Spirit against the flesh; these are opposed to each other, so that you may not do what you want.... [T]he fruit of the Spirit is love, joy, peace, patience, kindness, generosity, faithfulness, gentleness, self-control. Against such there is no law. Now those who belong to Christ [Jesus] have crucified their flesh with its passions and desires. If we live in the Spirit, let us also follow the Spirit. Let us not be conceited, provoking one another, envious of one another.

GALATIANS 5:16–17, 22–26

PRAYER

Dear God, how can I ever thank you for the graces you have showered upon me from the first moments of my existence? I know I cannot begin to name the persons, events, gifts, and talents you have designed to lead me by ways beyond my imagining to know you, love you, and serve you so as to fulfill the purpose for which you created me. At least now, let me learn to seek you through your beloved Son, Jesus Christ, that with him and in him I may truly understand what it means to call you Abba, Father! Amen.

ADVENT ACTION

Open your heart today to receive the gifts God is giving you through Christ to seek, recognize, and do the Father's will in peace and thankfulness.

DAY 14

WISDOM

The happy life is joy based on the truth. This is joy grounded in you, O God, who are the truth, my illumination, the salvation of my face, my God. This happy life everyone desires; joy in the truth everyone wants....They love the truth because they have no wish to be deceived, and when they love the happy life (which is none other than joy grounded in truth) they are unquestionably loving the truth....Why then do they not find their joy in this? Why are they not happy? It is because they are more occupied in other things.

CONFESSIONS, X, XXIII

SCRIPTURE

My child, from your youth choose discipline; and when you have gray hair you will find wisdom....Inquire and search, seek and find; when you get hold of her, do not let her go....If you wish, my [child], you can be wise; if you apply yourself, you can be shrewd. If you are willing to listen, you can learn; if you pay attention, you can be instructed. Stand in the company of the elders; stay close to whoever is wise. Be eager to hear every discourse; let no insightful saying escape you. If you see the intelligent, seek them out; let your feet wear away their doorsteps! Reflect on the law of the Most High, and let his commandments be your constant study. Then he will enlighten your mind, and make you wise as you desire.

SIRACH 6:18, 27, 32–37

PRAYER

Eternal, living God, it is you I seek with my whole heart. Through how many amazing ways do you look for me, scrutinize my mind and heart, bid me, call me, command me to turn to you, to walk with you, to find my joy and the secret of a happy life in what you will for me? Open my eyes to find you. Open my ears to hear your message in the silences I try to avoid. Amen.

ADVENT ACTION

Let this be a day when you seek to know the will of God in some situation that brings you face to face with what seems an insurmountable problem for you or someone you love.

WISDOM

My love for you, Lord, is not an uncertain feeling but a matter of conscious certainty. With your word you pierced my heart, and I loved you. But heaven and earth and everything in them on all sides tell me to love you....But when I love you, what do I love? It is not physical beauty nor temporal glory nor the brightness of light dear to earthly eyes, nor the sweet melodies of all kinds of songs, nor the gentle odor of flowers and ointments and perfumes, nor manna or honey, nor limbs welcoming the embraces of the flesh; it is not these I love when I love my God....

CONFESSIONS X, VIII

SCRIPTURE

Beloved, let us love one another, because love is of God; every-
one who loves is begotten by God and knows God. Whoever
is without love does not know God, for God is love. In this
way the love of God was revealed to us: God sent his only Son
into the world so that we might have life through him. In this
is love: not that we have loved God, but that he loved us and
sent his Son as expiation for our sins. Beloved, if God so loved
us, we also must love one another. No one has ever seen God.
Yet, if we love one another, God remains in us, and his love is
brought to perfection in us.

1 JOHN 4:7–12

PRAYER

God, you are love, and in the Incarnation of your beloved
Son you have revealed yourself as infinite, faithful, uncon-
ditional love. In contemplating his life and listening to his
teachings, we can learn the way in which we are graced
and enabled to respond to all that you will us to be. Mary,
his mother, the Mother of fair love, has been given to us as
a guide, a refuge, and a beacon in our efforts to follow a
Spirit-filled life. As the Infant Christ was taught by her to
embrace the fullness of human existence, so may we grow
in knowledge and love in our journey. Amen.

ADVENT ACTION

Let the love of God fill your heart and mind today, so that
you radiate the presence of Christ to everyone you meet.

DAY 16

WISDOM

What then do I love when I love my God? Who is he who is higher than the highest element in my soul? Through my soul I will ascend to him. I will rise above the force by which I am bonded to the body and fill its frame with vitality. It is not by that force that I find my God....There exists another power, not only that by which I give life to my body but also that by which I enable its senses to perceive....I will therefore rise above that natural capacity in a step-by-step ascent to him who made me.

CONFESSIONS X, VII

SCRIPTURE

I will sing of your mercy forever, LORD proclaim your faithfulness through all ages....The heavens praise your marvels, LORD, your loyalty in the assembly of the holy ones. Who in the skies ranks with the LORD? Who is like the LORD among the sons of the gods?....LORD, God of hosts, who is like you? Mighty LORD, your faithfulness surrounds you....You have a mighty arm. Your hand is strong; your right hand is ever exalted. Justice and judgment are the foundation of your throne; mercy and faithfulness march before you. Blessed the people who know the war cry, who walk in the radiance of your face, LORD.

PSALM 89:2, 6–7, 9, 14–16

PRAYER

Almighty and merciful God, we stand in awe before the splendor of your being. We know you as a Father who is stern with rebellious, wayward children. We know you as our Abba, ever ready to embrace us as we turn to you, asking forgiveness for our infidelities and straying. Eternal blessedness is the home to which you call us. Enlighten us to see the way you open before us, leading us surely to the eternal life of peace and love you have prepared for us. Amen.

ADVENT ACTION

Spend some time today in atonement for the failings that may be an obstacle between you and your loving Father. End the day in thanksgiving and praise for the mercies that are an assurance that you are cherished by a faithful God.

DAY 17

WISDOM

As for ourselves, we see the things you have made because they are. But they are because you see them. We see outwardly that they are, and inwardly that they are good. But you saw them made when you saw that it was right to make them....But you, God, one and good, have never ceased to do good. Of your gift we have some good works, though not everlasting. After them we hope to rest in your great sanctification. But you, the Good, in need of no other good, are ever at rest since you yourself are your own rest.

CONFESSIONS, XIII, XXXVIII

SCRIPTURE

I will extol you, my God and king; I will bless your name forever and ever. Every day I will bless you; I will praise your name forever and ever. Great is the LORD and worthy of much praise, whose grandeur is beyond understanding. One generation praises your deeds to the next and proclaims your mighty works. They speak of the splendor of your majestic glory, tell of your wonderful deeds. They speak of the power of your awesome acts and recount your great deeds. They celebrate your abounding goodness and joyfully sing of your justice. The LORD is gracious and merciful, slow to anger and abounding in mercy. The LORD is good to all, compassionate toward all your works.

PSALM 145:1–9

PRAYER

Lord, you never cease to surprise and amaze us with the prodigality of your works. It was not enough that you created all things seen and unseen. You continue in every age to pour out on women and men gifts and talents of nature and grace that astound us, open new horizons before us, and challenge us to use the riches you have entrusted to us for your glory and for the good of all. Open my eyes to see what lies in my hands and mind and heart to share with those who have need of what you have entrusted to me. Amen.

ADVENT ACTION

Try to find one person today who has need of some gift or talent confided to you and needed by that individual for comfort, consolation, or courage to face a difficult situation.

DAY 18

WISDOM

My God, give me yourself, restore yourself to me. See, I love you, and if it is too little, let me love you more strongly. I can conceive no measure by which to know how far my love falls short of that which is enough to make my life run to your embraces, and not to turn away until it lies hidden in the secret place of your presence. This alone I know: without you it is evil for me, not only in external things but within my being, and all my abundance which is other than my God is mere indigence....My weight is my love.

CONFESSIONS, XIII, VIII

SCRIPTURE

Hear, O Israel! The LORD is our God, the LORD alone! There-fore, you shall love the LORD, your God, with your whole heart, and with your whole being, and with your whole strength. Take to heart these words which I command you today. Keep repeating them to your children. Recite them when you are at home and when you are away, when you lie down and when you get up. Bind them on your arm as a sign and let them be as a pendant on your forehead. Write them on the doorposts of your houses and on your gates....The LORD, your God, shall you fear; him shall you serve.

DEUTERONOMY 6:4–8, 13

PRAYER

God of all times and places, I come before you to offer adoration, praise, love, and thanksgiving for all you are as Creator, Father, and center of my life. My desire to pray in this way can never be realized on my own. It is only through your Incarnate Word, the unborn Child in Mary's womb, that I am able to turn to you with all my heart and soul and strength. Your beloved Son is perfect adoration, praise, love, and gratitude. With him, I come to you and know I am em-braced as your adopted child. I rejoice in this blessing. Amen.

ADVENT ACTION

Let the joy of your experience as a beloved child of God overflow in acts of kindness and thoughtfulness today to everyone you meet.

✓ DAY 19

WISDOM

May I know you, who know me. May I "know as I also am known" (1 Corinthians 13:12). Power of my soul, enter into it and fit it for yourself, so that you may have and hold it "without spot or blemish" (Ephesians 5:27). This is my hope....In this hope I am placing my delight when my delight is in what it ought to be. As to the other pleasures of life, regret at their loss should be in inverse proportion to the extent to which one weeps for losing them....This I desire to do....

CONFESSIONS, X, 1

SCRIPTURE

Who is this who darkens counsel with words of ignorance?...I will question you, and you tell me the answers! Where were you when I founded the earth?...Have you ever in your lifetime commanded the morning and shown the dawn its place...? ...Have you entered into the sources of the sea, or walked about on the bottom of the deep? Have the gates of death been shown to you, or have you seen the gates of darkness? Have you comprehended the breadth of the earth?...Have you entered the storehouse of the snow, and seen the storehouses of the hail...?...Let him who would instruct God give answer!

JOB 38:2–4, 12, 16–18, 22; 40:2B

PRAYER

Infinite God, who can fathom the wonder of your perfections? We show the extent to which we have achieved the right to honor, recognition, and the flattery of others. We insist on letting everyone know the importance we have reached through our influence on others and the way our name is carved in places meant to preserve our fame. You did not refuse to come to earth and share our humanity. Teach us to know and accept the truth of who we are, dear humble God. Make our hearts like yours, dear God! Amen.

ADVENT ACTION

In company with the Incarnate Word in Mary's womb, today avoid calling attention to yourself in some area where you have recently gained recognition and achievement.

DAY 20

WISDOM

With you as my guide, I entered into my innermost citadel, and was given power to do so because you had become my helper (Psalm 29:11). I entered and with my soul's eye,....saw above that same eye of my soul the immutable light higher than my mind.... It was not that light, but a different thing, utterly different from all our kinds of light. It transcended my mind....It was superior because it made me, and I was inferior because I was made by it. The person who knows the truth knows it....Love knows it.

CONFESSIONS, VII, X

SCRIPTURE

Now will I recall God's works; what I have seen, I will describe....As the shining sun is clear to all, so the glory of the LORD fills all his works....He searches out the abyss and penetrates the heart; their secrets he understands. For the Most High possesses all knowledge, and sees from of old the things that are to come. He makes known the past and the future, and reveals the deepest secrets. He lacks no understanding; no single thing escapes him. He regulates the mighty deeds of his wisdom; he is from all eternity one and the same.

SIRACH 42:15–16, 18–21

PRAYER

God, your eternal Son became man, we are told, so we might become divine. He also became man so we might become truly human. In striving for both transformations, we travel the path traced out for us by the God-man and hope to become Christians, followers of Christ. What else does this mean, except to understand the meaning of a life marked by the Beatitudes: poverty of spirit, sorrow, meekness, hunger, and thirst for holiness, mercy, single-heartedness, peacefulness, and persecution. In all of this, grant that we be glad and joyful, for our reward is great in heaven. Amen.

ADVENT ACTION

Today choose one of the eight Beatitudes and find a way of expressing it in favor of someone you know who is facing a particularly challenging situation.

DAY 21

WISDOM

Lord God of truth, surely the person with a scientific knowledge of nature is not pleasing to you on that ground alone. The person who knows all those matters but is ignorant of you is unhappy. The person who knows you, even if ignorant of natural science, is happy....You alone are his source of happiness if knowing you he glorifies you for what you are and gives you thanks and is not lost in his own imagined ideas (Romans 1:21)....It is vanity to profess to know these scientific matters...; but it is piety to make confession to you.

CONFESSIONS, V, IV

The wisdom of the poor lifts their head high and sets them among princes....Good and evil, life and death, poverty and riches—all are from the LORD....The Lord's gift remains with the devout; his favor brings lasting success. Some become rich through a miser's life....When they say: "I have found rest, now I will feast on my goods," they do not know how long it will be till they die and leave them to others....[T]rust in the LORD and wait for his light....God's blessing is the lot of the righteous, and in due time their hope bears fruit.

SIRACH 11:1, 14, 17–19, 21–22

PRAYER

All-knowing God, so often I resist venturing into fields of interest to the human mind because of the challenge of intellectual effort. It is easier to settle for zones of comfort that have been familiar to me. At times I take refuge in the claim that I prefer to spend my energies on spiritual realities rather than on the confusions of modern science or technology. Open my eyes to see that everything of importance to the mind is a way to deeper friendship and love of you. Amen.

ADVENT ACTION

Stretch your mind today by seeking to learn something outside your ordinary interests, as a tribute to God, who knows all things and who desires that we continue to pursue every avenue of truth, so as to grow in knowledge of our wonderful God, who is infinite truth.

WISDOM

*Prepare the way for the Lord....*To prepare the way means to pray well; it means thinking humbly of oneself. We should take our lesson from John the Baptist. He is thought to be the Christ; he declares he is not what they think. He does not take advantage of their mistake to further his own glory....He pointed out clearly who he was; he humbled himself. He saw where his salvation lay. He understood that he was a lamp, and his fear was that it might be blown out by the wind of pride.

SERMON 293, 3

SCRIPTURE

When John heard in prison of the works of the Messiah, he sent his disciples to him with this question, "Are you the one who is to come, or should we look for another?" Jesus said to them in reply, "Go and tell John what you hear and see: the blind regain their sight, the lame walk, lepers are cleansed, the deaf hear, the dead are raised, and the poor have the good news proclaimed to them. And blessed is the one who takes no offense at me." As they were going off, Jesus began to speak to the crowds about John:..."Amen, I say to you, among those born of women there has been none greater than John the Baptist; yet the least in the kingdom of heaven is greater than he."

MATTHEW 11:2–7, 11

PRAYER

Great God of our lives! What can we learn from your Son's precursor, if not humility? How easy it is to look for ways to "increase" our name, our fame, our prestige through boasting of the achievements and honors that have come to us. What is the merit of all that? Jesus affirmed that no one born of woman was greater than John. He also declared that entrance into the kingdom of his Father surpassed even that. Grant me the grace to "decrease" and seek the only title I ought to desire: that of being a Christian. Amen.

ADVENT ACTION

Avoid announcing today some recognition that has come to you recently as a means of sharing the "decreasing" of John the Baptizer, so that Christ may "increase" in your life.

DAY 23

WISDOM

As the earth produces her fruit, so at your command, the command of its Lord God, our soul yields works of mercy "according to its kind" (Genesis 1:12), loving our neighbor in the relief of physical necessities....Aware of our own infirmity we are moved to compassion to help the indigent, assisting them in the same way as we would wish to be helped if we were in the same distress—and not only in easy ways....This means such kindness as rescuing a person suffering injustice from the hand of the powerful and providing the shelter of protection by the mighty force of just judgment.

CONFESSIONS, XIII, XVIII

SCRIPTURE

You shall not oppress or afflict a resident alien, for you were once aliens residing in the land of Egypt. You shall not wrong any widow or orphan....If you lend money to my people, the poor among you, you must not be like a money lender; you must not demand interest from them....You shall not repeat a false report. Do not join your hand with the wicked to be a witness supporting violence. You shall not follow the crowd in doing wrong. When testifying in a lawsuit, you shall not follow the crowd in perverting justice....You shall not pervert justice for the needy among you in a lawsuit. You shall keep away from anything dishonest. The innocent and the just you shall not put to death, for I will not acquit the guilty.

EXODUS 22:20–21, 24; 23:1–2, 6–7

PRAYER

Most just and merciful God, you know the dust of which we are made and our weakness in striving to do good. All around us we see those who seek their own advantage at the expense of others. We bemoan the wrongs exposed in the media and praise those whose integrity shines out. As for ourselves, we stand on the sidelines and hesitate to step forward rather than act. Give us the courage of our convictions! Open our eyes to the opportunities around us. Amen.

ADVENT ACTION

What one deed can you do today to right a wrong, defend someone unjustly accused, or assist a needy person?

DAY 24

WISDOM

Your Word, eternal truth, higher than the superior parts of your creation, raises those submissive to him to himself. In the inferior parts he built for himself a humble house of our clay. By this he detaches from themselves those who are willing to be made his subjects and carries them across to himself, healing their swelling and nourishing their love. They are no longer to place confidence in themselves, but rather to become weak. They see at their feet divinity become weak by his sharing in our "coat of skin" (Genesis 3:21). In their weariness they fall prostrate before this divine weakness which rises and lifts them up.

CONFESSIONS, VII, XVIII

SCRIPTURE

In "subjecting" all things to [Christ], [God] left nothing not "subject to him." Yet at present we do not see "all things subject to him," but we do see Jesus "crowned with glory and honor" because he suffered death, he who "for a little while" was made "lower than the angels," that by the grace of God he might taste death for everyone. For it was fitting that he, for whom and through whom all things exist, in bringing many children to glory, should make the leader to their salvation perfect through suffering....Now since the children share in blood and flesh, he likewise shared in them, that through death he might destroy the...devil, and free those who through fear of death had been subject to slavery all their life.

HEBREWS 2:8–10, 14–15

PRAYER

Gracious Father, we stand in awe and wonder at the amazing way in which you foresaw, from all eternity, the redemption of sinful humanity through the Incarnation of your beloved Son. We contemplate the priceless gifts of his life, ministry, passion, and death, offered for us. We praise the power and glory of his triumphant resurrection with its assurance of the strength to remain faithful to the graces that will lead us to an eternal life with you after this earthly exile. Amen.

ADVENT ACTION

Resolve to draw on the power of Christ's resurrection to help you face a difficult situation that challenges you.

DAY 25

WISDOM

What can I say in praise of charity that surpasses in grandeur what the Lord thunders forth through the mouth of his apostle, as he shows us a more excellent way....It tolerates all things, believes all things, hopes all things, endures all things. Charity never falls away. What a great thing this charity is! The soul of the scriptures, the force of prophecy, the saving power of the sacraments, the fruit of faith, the wealth of the poor, the life of the dying. What could be more magnanimous than to die for the godless, what more kindly than to love one's enemies?

SERMON 350, 3

SCRIPTURE

If I speak in human and angelic tongues but do not have love, I am a resounding gong or a clashing cymbal. And if I have the gift of prophecy and comprehend all mysteries and all knowledge; if I have all faith so as to move mountains but do not have love, I am nothing. If I give away everything I own, and if I hand my body over so that I may boast but do not have love, I gain nothing.... [Love] bears all things, believes all things, hopes all things, endures all things. So faith, hope, love remain, these three; but the greatest of these is love.

1 CORINTHIANS 13:1–3, 7, 13

PRAYER

Loving God, it would seem that it is too easy to be called to live the heart of the Gospel through the simple commandment of love. Yet how is it possible to love you, my God, and to love my neighbor as myself? For so many years, this has been my goal. I begin again, over and over, turning my whole heart, my whole soul, and all my mind to this end, only to fail again and again. Help me realize that it is only with, in, and through Jesus the Lord that I can learn to love as you would have and strive to attain the perfection of charity for your praise and glory. Amen.

ADVENT ACTION

Go out of your way today to live the Great Commandment in favor of some person you meet or live with.

DAY 26

WISDOM

O Lord our God, under the covering of your wings (Exodus 19:4) we set our hope. Protect us and bear us up. It is you who will carry us; you will bear us up from our infancy until old age (Isaiah 46:4). When you are our firm support, then it is firm indeed. But when our support rests on our own strength, it is infirmity. Our good is life with you for ever, and because we turned away from that, we became twisted. Let us now return to you....Our good is life with you and suffers no deficiency; for you yourself are that good.

CONFESSIONS, IV, XVI

SCRIPTURE

How can I repay the LORD for all the great good done for me?
I will raise the cup of salvation and call on the name of the
LORD. LORD, I am your servant, your servant, the child of your
maidservant; you have loosed my bonds. I will offer a sacrifice
of praise and call on the name of the LORD.

PSALM 116:12–13, 16–17

PRAYER

Dear Father, from our youth we learn that we are to pray to
you with words of adoration, praise, love, repentance, and
thanksgiving. Today I come to bless and glorify your name,
your holy being, your might and everlasting kindness. All
that is good in my life has been your freely granted gift.
Without your mercy and goodness, I could not draw one
breath of life. Thank you for your patient understanding
and the gentleness with which you cherish me from day to
day and lead me through every challenge. Thank you for the
gift of Jesus, your Incarnate Word, through whom your give
me everything I need. Amen.

ADVENT ACTION

The next time you meet someone who has not recognized
God's goodness in his or her life, try to open that person's
eyes to the marvels of God's love.

✓ DAY 27

WISDOM

Your works praise you that we may love you, and we love you that your works may praise you. They have a beginning and an end in time, a rise and a fall, a start and a finish, beauty and the loss of it. They have in succession a morning and an evening, in part hidden, in part evident. They are made out of nothing by you, not from you, not from some matter not of your making or previously existing, but from matter created by you together with its form....The matter of heaven and earth is one thing, the beauty of heaven and earth is another.

CONFESSIONS, XIII, XXXIII

SCRIPTURE

The heavens declare the glory of God; the firmament proclaims the works of his hands. Day unto day pours forth speech; night unto night whispers knowledge. There is no speech, no words; their voice is not heard; a report goes forth through all the earth, their messages, to the ends of the world....The law of the LORD is perfect, refreshing the soul. The decree of the LORD is trustworthy, giving wisdom to the simple. The precepts of the LORD are right, rejoicing the heart. The command of the LORD is clear, enlightening the eye. The fear of the LORD is pure, enduring forever.

PSALM 19:2–5, 8–10

PRAYER

Dear Lord, Creator of all that is, you have established all things for our wonder and delight, and we are grateful. But as we contemplate your works, we know that their goodness and beauty come from their submission to your will and design. Grant that we, your adopted daughters and sons, alone may not betray the purpose for which you have created, chosen, and loved us, setting us over the works of your hands so they may be used always for your glory. Amen.

ADVENT ACTION

Take time today to relish the beauty of this season with its reminders of the fruit of the days that have gone before us and its promise of the good things to come, as this season pursues its way to the wondrous birth of the Incarnate Word.

DAY 28

WISDOM

Awake, mankind! For your sake God has become man. *Awake, you who sleep, rise up from the dead, and Christ will enlighten you.* I tell you again: for your sake, God has become man. You would have suffered eternal death, had he not been born in time. Never would you have been freed from sinful flesh, had he not taken on himself the likeness of sinful flesh. You would have suffered everlasting unhappiness, had it not been for this mercy. You would never have returned to life, had he not shared your death. You would have been lost if he had not hastened to your aid. You would have perished, had he not come.

SERMON 185

SCRIPTURE

For when peaceful stillness encompassed everything and the night in its swift course was half spent, Your all-powerful word from heaven's royal throne leapt into the doomed land, a fierce warrior bearing the sharp sword of your inexorable decree, and alighted, and filled every place with death, and touched heaven, while standing upon the earth....Yet not for long did the anger last. For the blameless man hastened to be their champion, bearing the weapon of his special office, prayer and the propitiation of incense; He withstood the wrath and put a stop to the calamity, showing that he was your servant.

WISDOM 18:14–16, 20–21

PRAYER

Father, the Advent days have come to an end and we await, on this holy night, the celebration of the appearance on earth of your beloved Son, Jesus the Christ. He comes with every blessing, with every mercy, with every good gift that you will for us, dear God. Now, at last, let mountains be laid low and rough ways plain, and every path before us be made straight to lead us with your beloved Child to the fulfillment of your grace-filled promises. Amen.

ADVENT ACTION

Spend time today in joyful gratitude for the coming of the Child of Mary, the eternal Son of the Father, Jesus, to begin once again the peaceful revolution that, in the power of the Spirit, will renew the face of our weary world.

PART II

~

READINGS
for the
CHRISTMAS
SEASON

DAY 1

WISDOM

This is the birthday of our Lord and Savior Jesus Christ. It is the anniversary of the day on which...the Day of Day was born to bring light into our day. It is a day we ought to celebrate.... Our Christian faith alone can convey to us what this sublime act of humility gave to us. It is something that utterly escapes the understanding of unbelievers; because God has hidden these things from the wise and prudent....Let the humble, therefore, make God's humility their own. With help such as this, with this to carry, as it were, the burden of their weakness, they will arrive at the sublimity of God.

SERMON 2, 1

SCRIPTURE

The LORD says to my lord: "Sit at my right hand, while I make your enemies your footstool." The scepter of your might: the LORD extends your strong scepter from Zion. Have dominion over your enemies! Yours is princely power from the day of your birth. In holy splendor before the daystar, like dew I begot you. The Lord has sworn and will not waver: "You are a priest forever in the manner of Melchizedek." At your right hand is the Lord, who crushes kings on the day of his wrath....Who drinks from the brook by the wayside and thus holds high his head.

PSALM 110:1–5, 7

PRAYER

Father, on this day in a most unique way, we call you by this name that tells us who the Child born in Bethlehem is: your beloved Son. This day is hallowed as no other day, and we are made holy with it, as we realize that we, too, can call you "Father." As we claim our blessings as your sons and daughters, grant us the grace to imitate the humility of Jesus. It is only in this way that we can hope to share his glory. Amen.

CHRISTMAS ACTION

Let this day be one of grateful joy as you celebrate the birthday of our Lord Jesus Christ and praise God for this gracious gift of the Incarnate Word, whose presence renews the earth.

DAY 2

WISDOM

Let us...celebrate the Lord's birthday with the full attendance and the enthusiasm that we should give it. Let men rejoice, let women rejoice....Rejoice, you who are just. It is the birthday of Him who justifies. Rejoice, you who are weak and sick. It is the birthday of Him who makes well. Rejoice, you who are in captivity. It is the birthday of the Redeemer. Rejoice, you who are slaves. It is the birthday of the Master. Rejoice, you who are free. It is the birthday of Him who makes free. Rejoice, you Christians all. It is Christ's birthday.

SERMON 2, 2

SCRIPTURE

It is good to give thanks to the LORD, to sing praise to your name, Most High, to proclaim your love at daybreak, your faithfulness in the night, with the ten-stringed harp, with melody upon the lyre. For you make me jubilant, LORD, by your deeds; at the works of your hands I shout for joy. How great are your works, LORD! How profound your designs! A senseless person cannot know this; a fool cannot comprehend....The just shall flourish like the palm tree, shall grow like a cedar of Lebanon. Planted in the house of the LORD, they shall flourish in the courts of our God.

PSALM 92:2–7, 13–14

PRAYER

Gracious God, into this world of ours, with its turmoil, unrest, and threats to all we hold dear you have sent your Son, the Prince of Peace, the Lord of love and kindliness, the Savior who brings healing and hope with his coming. There is reason, here, for me to rejoice, to give thanks, and to praise you, dear God, in and with Jesus the Christ, in the power of your Holy Spirit. Amen.

CHRISTMAS ACTION

Today place all your worries and concerns into the hands of the Child born in Bethlehem. Trust his love to care for you and those dear to you.

✓ **DAY 3**

WISDOM

By His birth of an earthborn mother He hallowed this one day who by His birth of the Father was the Creator of all ages. In the one birth a mother was impossible, while for the other no human father was required. In fact, Christ was born both of a father and of a mother, both without a father and without a mother; of a father as God, of a mother as man; without a mother as God, without a father as man. The one is without time, the other without seed; the one without beginning, the other without parallel; the one which has always been, the other which has never been before or since; the one which does not end, the other which begins where it ends.

SERMON 2, 3

SCRIPTURE

In the sixth month, the angel Gabriel was sent from God to a town of Galilee called Nazareth, to a virgin betrothed to a man named Joseph, of the house of David, and the virgin's name was Mary. And coming to her, he said, "Hail, favored one! The Lord is with you." But she was greatly troubled at what was said and pondered what sort of greeting this might be. Then the angel said to her, "Do not be afraid, Mary, for you have found favor with God. Behold, you will conceive in your womb and bear a son, and you shall name him Jesus. He will be great and will be called Son of the Most High."

LUKE 1:26–32, 35

PRAYER

Dear God, to make certain that your Incarnate Word would be like us in all things but sin, you sent him into this world in the manner that every human being comes to be. You chose for him a mother unique in all the world, but still a woman like every other woman. To affirm this likeness with us, you chose a man, Joseph the just, to be on earth the image of your own Fatherhood. Bless all families who look to the one we call "holy" and give them the grace they need to be faithful to their call. Amen.

CHRISTMAS ACTION

Today, give thanks to the Lord for the blessings you have received through the parents God has given you.

✓ DAY 4

WISDOM

See...what God has become for you. Take to heart the lesson
of this great humility, though the Teacher of it is still without
speech. Once, in Paradise, you were so eloquent that you gave a
name to every living being; but your Creator, because of you, lay
speechless, and did not call even his mother by her name. You,
finding yourself in a boundless estate of fruitful groves, destroyed
yourself by having no regard for obedience; He, obedient, came
as a mortal man to a poor, tiny lodging that by dying He might
seek the return of him who had died.

SERMON 6, 3

SCRIPTURE

[W]hen you come to serve the Lord, prepare yourself for trials. Be sincere of heart and steadfast, and do not be impetuous in time of adversity. Cling to him, do not leave him, that you may prosper in your last days. Accept whatever happens to you; in periods of humiliation be patient. For in fire gold is tested, and the chosen, in the crucible of humiliation. Trust in God, and he will help you; make your ways straight and hope in him. You that fear the Lord, wait for his mercy....You that fear the Lord, trust in him, and your reward will not be lost.

SIRACH 2:1–8

PRAYER

Provident God, in your will to rescue the human race from the misery into which we had fallen, you sent a "second Adam" to sum up and redeem the sin of the first Adam, and to bring us all into the blessing and reconciliation of new life in Christ. We are grateful for this new creation that has been granted us through the graces of the sacramental life of the Church through which your Son continues to call us to you. In him and with him, we desire to live according to your will, for the praise and glory of your name. Amen.

CHRISTMAS ACTION

Live this day in the spirit of your baptism and in gratitude for the life of Christ which you share.

✓ **DAY 5**

WISDOM

Let the world, therefore, rejoice in those who believe. To save them, He came through whom the world was made—the Creator of Mary, born of Mary; the Son of David, Lord of David; the seed of Abraham, who was before Abraham; the Maker of the earth, made on the earth; He who brought the heavens into existence, brought into existence under the heavens. He Himself is the day which the Lord hath made, and the day of our heart is itself the Lord. Let us walk in His light, let us rejoice and take delight in it.

SERMON 5, 4

SCRIPTURE

[F]rom now on we regard no one according to the flesh....So whoever is in Christ is a new creation: the old things have passed away; behold, new things have come. And all this is from God, who has reconciled us to himself through Christ and given us the ministry of reconciliation, namely, God was reconciling the world to himself in Christ, not counting their trespasses against them and entrusting to us the message of reconciliation. So we are ambassadors for Christ, as if God were appealing through us. We implore you on behalf of Christ, be reconciled to God. For our sake he made him to be sin who did not know sin, so that we might become the righteousness of God in him.

2 CORINTHIANS 5:16–21

PRAYER

Wonderful God, when I reflect on the abundance of gifts you have showered upon me from the beginning of my life, I am overcome with awe. Nothing I have received from you has been due to my own merit or worthiness. Indeed, I am worthy because of you and your gifts. The greatest of these, I know, is the gift of your beloved Child, Jesus. He is the joy of my heart, the light of my life, the strength I need to seek always to do your will and serve those you would have me serve. May you be praised forever. Amen.

CHRISTMAS ACTION

Recognize today some person whom God calls you to serve, out of love for the newborn Child of Bethlehem.

DAY 6

WISDOM

What signal dignity has been conferred on us! What indignation had gone before! How did this His indignation show itself? We were mortal, we were bearing the load of our sins, we were burdened down by our punishments. Every human being at birth begins life with misery. Do not consult the Prophet about this—ask the infant when it is born, look how it cries!...And what is this dignity conferred all of a sudden?...Christ has been born; let no one hesitate to be reborn. Christ has been begotten, but without need of being begotten anew. Indeed, for whom was a second begetting necessary, if not for him whose first begetting was condemned? May His mercy, therefore, be given to our hearts.

SERMON 7, 3

SCRIPTURE

[A]Pharisee named Nicodemus, a ruler of the Jews...came to Jesus at night and said to him, "Rabbi, we know that you are a teacher who has come from God, for no one can do these signs that you are doing unless God is with him." Jesus answered and said to him, "Amen, amen, I say to you, no one can see the kingdom of God without being born from above." Nicodemus said to him, "How can a person once grown old be born again? Surely he cannot reenter his mother's womb and be born again, can he?" Jesus answered, "Amen, amen, I say to you, no one can enter the kingdom of God without being born of water and Spirit."

JOHN 3:1–5

PRAYER

Loving Father Abba, during these days of celebrating the birth in human time of your beloved Son, we are called to ponder the mystery of the shadow of the cross that already marks the scene at Bethlehem. We know the name given by the prophet to the Child we call Jesus. He is to be the suffering servant whose death will release us from all burdens. Through his death, our rebirth is promised and realized. Through his suffering, we enter the land of true joy. May this be so! Amen.

CHRISTMAS ACTION

Resist all temptations to discouragement and sadness today; enter into God's joy!

DAY 7

WISDOM

Our Lord Jesus, who was with His Father before He was born of His mother, chose not only the virgin from whom He was to be born, but also the day on which He was to be born. Misguided men very frequently go by certain dates. One man chooses a day for setting out new vines; another, a day for building; another, a day for starting on a journey; and sometimes, too, a man takes a special day for getting married....But no one is able to choose the day of his own birth; whereas the Lord, who was able to create both, was also able to choose both.

SERMON 8, 1

SCRIPTURE

In the beginning was the Word, and the Word was with God, and the Word was God. He was in the beginning with God. All things came to be through him, and without him nothing came to be. What came to be through him was life, and this life was the light of the human race; the light shines in the darkness, and the darkness has not overcome it....He was in the world, and the world came to be through him, but the world did not know him....From his fullness we have all received, grace in place of grace, because while the law was given through Moses, grace and truth came through Jesus Christ. No one has ever seen God. The only Son, God, who is at the Father's side, has revealed him.

JOHN 1:1–5, 10, 16–18

PRAYER

Eternal God, with the dawn of Christmas Day we are blessed with the light to radiate hope and enthusiasm for every day. In this holy light, we have the vision to see the way in which we are to walk, living in the grace of the kingdom, proclaiming that Christ has come, preparing for the day when he will come again. This is our hope. This is the gift we affirm. This is the source of our faithfulness to you. Amen.

CHRISTMAS ACTION

Celebrate this holy season in some special way today, and invite someone to share it with you.

✓ DAY 8

WISDOM

Placed in a manger, He became our food. In the two animals, let two people approach the manger:...Look at the manger: do not be ashamed to be the Lord's beast of burden. You will be bearing Christ, you will not go astray as you go your way; the Way is sitting upon you! Do you recall the ass's foal that was brought to the Lord? Let no one blush—we are that. Let the Lord sit upon us, and let Him direct us whither He will. Let us be His beast of burden....With Him leading us on, we shall not go astray.

SERMON 7, 4

SCRIPTURE

Hear, O heavens, and listen, O earth, for the LORD speaks: Sons have I raised and reared, but they have rebelled against me! An ox knows its owner, and an ass, its master's manger. But Israel does not know, my people have not understood....Put away your misdeeds from before my eyes; cease doing evil;learn to do good. Make justice your aim: redress the wronged, hear the orphan's plea, defend the widow. Come now, let us set things right, says the LORD: Though your sins be like scarlet, they may become white as snow...If you are willing, and obey, you shall eat the good things of the land.

ISAIAH 1:2–3, 16–19

PRAYER

Creator God, we are the work of your hands, living witnesses to your love. Of all creatures on earth, we are the only ones who can defy your will. We are also the only ones through whom all other creatures can praise you fittingly. This is so because of Jesus, the only one who can give you perfect praise, perfect adoration, perfect obedience. Grant us the grace to be configured to his likeness in the Spirit so we may offer you a life pleasing to you. Amen.

CHRISTMAS ACTION

Live today in thanksgiving for the great gift of a life that is transformed each time you choose to be like Christ in thought, word, or deed. Choose one specific action of Christ-likeness toward one other person today.

DAY 9

WISDOM

[Beloved], let us be happy! Let the nations rejoice and exult!
Not the visible sun, but the sun's invisible Creator gave us this
holy day, when the Virgin Mother, from the fruitfulness of her
womb and with her virginity preserved, brought forth Him who
was made visible for us and by whom—invisible—she herself
had been created. A virgin who conceives, a virgin who gives
birth; a virgin with Child, a virgin delivered of Child—a virgin
ever virgin! Why do you marvel at these things...? When God
vouchsafed to become man, it was fitting that He should be born
in this way. He who was made of her had made her what she was.

SERMON 4, 1

SCRIPTURE

Who can find a woman of worth? Far beyond jewels is her value....She seeks out wool and flax and weaves with skillful hands....She picks out a field and acquires it; from her earnings she plants a vineyard....She reaches out her hands to the poor, and extends her arms to the needy....She is clothed with strength and dignity, and laughs at the days to come. She opens her mouth in wisdom; kindly instruction is on her tongue. She watches over the affairs of her household, and does not eat the bread of idleness. Her children rise up and call her blessed; her husband, too, praises her: "Many are the women of proven worth, but you have excelled them all." Charm is deceptive and beauty fleeting; the woman who fears the LORD is to be praised.

PROVERBS 31:10, 13, 16, 20, 25–30

PRAYER

God, source of all joy, in our enthusiasm for the blessings of this holy season, we readily join in the angels' joy of praise: *Gloria in excelsis Deo—Glory to God in the highest!* Yet, we know that Christmas is the beginning of a story that points to another feast: the day of resurrection. As we sing with the angels, let us remember we are called to be *an Easter people. Alleluia is our song!* Amen.

CHRISTMAS ACTION

Choose one of your favorite Christmas hymns to sing to the Christ Child today.

DAY 10

WISDOM

When we were living without faith, we were night. And, because this same lack of faith which covered the whole world like the night had to be lessened by the growth of faith, so on the birthday of our Lord Jesus Christ the nights began to be shorter, while the days became longer. Let us, therefore..., keep this day with due solemnity; not like those who are without faith, on account of the sun, but because of Him who made the sun. For He who was the Word, was made flesh, that for our sakes He might be under the sun. Under the sun, to be sure, in His flesh, but in His majesty, over the whole universe in which he made the sun.

SERMON 8

SCRIPTURE

[N]ow in Christ Jesus you who once were far off have become near by the blood of Christ. For he is our peace....He came and preached peace to you who were far off....So then you are no longer strangers and sojourners, but you are fellow citizens with the holy ones and members of the household of God, built upon the foundation of the apostles and prophets, with Christ Jesus himself as the capstone. Through him the whole structure is held together and grows into a temple sacred in the Lord; in him you also are being built together into a dwelling place of God in the Spirit.

EPHESIANS 2:13–14, 17, 19–22

PRAYER

God of Peace and every good gift, we celebrate the coming of your beloved Child, the Prince of Peace. This is his will, as it is yours: that peace reign on the earth, that humankind renounce violence and war, that your family be established in every nation and among all peoples. We pray for the coming of this peace. We commit ourselves to strive for reconciliation and the end to divisions. Let this begin with me. Amen.

CHRISTMAS ACTION

Try to make one act of peace that will promote the reconciliation of someone you know who lives in a state of alienation or separation from a loved one. If you are unable to act, spend time in prayer for this intention.

DAY 11

WISDOM

[B]ecause He Himself certainly had created both sexes, that is, male and female, even by His being born He wished to honor the sexes which He had come to free. [T]he Lord, coming to seek what had been lost, wished to honor and distinguish both, because both had been lost. Regarding neither sex, therefore, ought we to affront the Creator; both have been favored by the Lord's Nativity with the hope of salvation. The honor of the male sex comes from the body of Christ; the honor of the female sex is in the mother of Christ. The grace of Jesus Christ has won over the cunning of the serpent.

SERMON 8, 2

SCRIPTURE

Why, then, the law? It was added for transgressions, until the descendant came to whom the promise had been made....Before faith came, we were held in custody under law, confined for the faith that was to be revealed. Consequently, the law was our disciplinarian for Christ, that we might be justified by faith. But now that faith has come, we are no longer under a disciplinarian. For through faith you are all children of God in Christ Jesus. For all of you who were baptized into Christ have clothed yourselves with Christ. There is neither Jew nor Greek, there is neither slave nor free person, there is not male and female; for you are all one in Christ Jesus.

GALATIANS 3:19, 23–28

PRAYER

Dear God, how much we humans desire freedom! Our idea of it, however, is often at odds with our responsibilities both as humans and as followers of Christ and members of your family. We pray for the grace and the wisdom to understand the full meaning of Gospel freedom. We pray, especially, to strive to surrender ourselves with open hands and hearts to be slaves of Christ. With, in, and through Christ, we desire to be slaves of your will and love, dear Father. Amen.

CHRISTMAS ACTION

Examine your conscience today to identify one area in which you continue to resist Gospel freedom and hold to your own will.

DAY 12

WISDOM

Whence is peace on earth, if not from the fact that Truth is sprung out of the earth, that is, Christ is born of flesh?....

Let us, then, rejoice in this grace, that our glory may be the testimony of our conscience, wherein we may glory, not in ourselves, but in the Lord....For what greater grace could have dawned upon us from God, than that He, who had only one Son, made Him the son of man, and so in turn made the son of man a son of God. Ask yourself whether this involved any merit, any motivation, any right on your part; and see whether you find anything but grace!

SERMON 3, 3

SCRIPTURE

Blessed be the God and Father of our Lord Jesus Christ, who has blessed us in Christ with every spiritual blessing in the heavens, as he chose us in him, before the foundation of the world, to be holy and without blemish before him. In love he destined us for adoption to himself through Jesus Christ, in accord with the favor of his will, for the praise of the glory of his grace that he granted us in the beloved. In him we have redemption by his blood, the forgiveness of transgressions, in accord with the riches of his grace that he lavished upon us.

EPHESIANS 1:3–8

PRAYER

Gracious God, as we come to the end of the Christmas season, I give thanks for having gone to Bethlehem with the humble shepherds to see the wonder announced by the angels. I offer the Lamb of God the little things that mark my life, just as they brought their sheep. I follow the star that guides me with the wise men to lay at the feet of the little king the fruit of my talents, just as they gave the riches of their lives. May all I have, your gifts to me, be at his service and for your glory. Amen.

CHRISTMAS ACTION

Spend time before the Christmas crib today to contemplate the Incarnate Son of God with Mary, Joseph, the shepherds, and the Magi. Ask the Child for the gift he wishes to give you.

PART III

FORMATS for NIGHTLY PRAYER and READING

Formats for
Nightly Prayer and Reading

$\mathcal{T}$HE PURPOSE OF PRESENTING two optional formats for nightly reading and prayer is to offer ways to use the material in this book for group or individual prayer. Of course, there are other ways in which to use this book—for example, as a meditative daily reader or as a guide for a prayer journal—but the following familiar liturgical formats provide a structure that can be used in a variety of contexts.

FORMAT 1

OPENING PRAYER

The observance begins with these words:

God, come to my assistance.
Lord, make haste to help me.

Followed by:

Glory to the Father, and to the Son,
and to the Holy Spirit, as it was in the beginning,
is now, and will be for ever. Amen. Alleluia.

EXAMINATION OF CONSCIENCE

If this observance is being prayed individually, an examination of conscience may be included. Here is a short examination of conscience; you may, of course, use your own method.

1. Place yourself in a quiet frame of mind.

2. Review your life since your last confession.

3. Reflect on the Ten Commandments and any sins against these commandments.

4. Reflect on the words of the Gospel, especially Jesus' commandment to love your neighbor as yourself.

5. Ask yourself these questions:
   Have I been unkind in thoughts, words, and actions?
   Am I refusing to forgive anyone?
   Do I despise any group or person?
   Am I a prisoner of fear, anxiety, worry, guilt, inferiority, or hatred of myself?

PENITENTIAL RITE (OPTIONAL)

If a group of people are praying in unison, a penitential rite from *the Roman Missal* may be used:

Presider: You were sent to heal the contrite of heart:
Lord, have mercy.

All: Lord, have mercy.

Presider: You came to call sinners:
Christ, have mercy.

All: Christ, have mercy.

Presider: You are seated at the right hand of the Father
to intercede for us:
Lord, have mercy.

All: Lord, have mercy.

Presider: May almighty God have mercy on us, forgive us
our sins, and bring us to everlasting life.

All: Amen.

HYMN: "O COME, O COME, EMMANUEL"

A hymn is now sung or recited. This Advent hymn is a paraphrase of the great "O" Antiphons, written in the twelfth century and translated by John Mason Neale in 1852.

O come, O come, Emmanuel,
And ransom captive Israel;
That mourns in lonely exile here,
Until the Son of God appear.

Refrain: Rejoice! Rejoice! O Israel,
To thee shall come Emmanuel!

O come, thou wisdom, from on high,
And order all things far and nigh;
To us the path of knowledge show,
And teach us in her ways to go. (*Refrain*)

O come, O come, thou Lord of might,
Who to thy tribes on Sinai's height
In ancient times did give the law,
In cloud, and majesty, and awe. (*Refrain*)

O come, thou rod of Jesse's stem,
From ev'ry foe deliver them
That trust thy mighty power to save,
And give them vict'ry o'er the grave. (*Refrain*)

O come, thou key of David, come,
And open wide our heav'nly home,
Make safe the way that leads on high,
That we no more have cause to sigh. (*Refrain*)

O come, thou Dayspring from on high,
And cheer us by thy drawing nigh;
Disperse the gloomy clouds of night
And death's dark shadow put to flight. (*Refrain*)

O come, Desire of nations, bind
In one the hearts of all mankind;
Bid every strife and quarrel cease
And fill the world with heaven's peace. (*Refrain*)

PSALM 27:7–14 GOD STANDS BY US IN DANGERS

Hear my voice, LORD, when I call;
    have mercy on me and answer me.
"Come," says my heart, "seek his face";
    your face, LORD, do I seek!
Do not hide your face from me;
    do not repel your servant in anger.
You are my salvation; do not cast me off;
    do not forsake me, God my savior!
Even if my father and mother forsake me,
    the LORD will take me in.
LORD, show me your way;
    lead me on a level path
    because of my enemies.
Do not abandon me to the desire of my foes;
    malicious and lying witnesses have risen against me.
I believe I shall see the LORD's goodness
    in the land of the living.
Wait for the LORD, take courage;
    be stouthearted, wait for the LORD!

RESPONSE

I long to see your face, O Lord.
You are my light and my help.
Do not turn away from me.

SCRIPTURE READING

Read silently or have a presider proclaim the Scripture
of the day that is selected.

RESPONSE

Come and set us free, Lord God of power and might.
Let your face shine on us and we will be saved.

> *Glory to the Father, and to the Son,*
> *and to the Holy Spirit:*
> *as it was in the beginning, is now,*
> *and will be for ever. Amen.*

SECOND READING

Read silently or have a presider read the words of
St. Augustine for the day selected.

CANTICLE OF SIMEON

Lord, now you let your servant go in peace;
    your word has been fulfilled:
my own eyes have seen the salvation
    which you have prepared in the sight of every people:
a light to reveal you to the nations
    and the glory of your people Israel.

Glory to the Father, and to the Son, and to the Holy Spirit:
as it was in the beginning, is now,
and will be for ever. Amen.

PRAYER

Recite the prayer that follows the excerpt from
St. Augustine for the day selected.

BLESSING

May the all-powerful Lord grant us a restful night
and a peaceful death. Amen.

MARIAN ANTIPHON

Loving mother of the Redeemer,
gate of heaven, star of the sea,
assist your people who have fallen yet strive to rise again.
To the wonderment of nature you bore your Creator,
yet remained a virgin after as before.
You who received Gabriel's joyful greeting,
have pity on us poor sinners.

FORMAT 2

OPENING PRAYER

The observance begins with these words:

God, come to my assistance.
Lord, make haste to help me.

Followed by:

Glory to the Father, and to the Son,
and to the Holy Spirit, as it was in the beginning,
is now, and will be for ever. Amen. Alleluia.

Examination of Conscience

If this observance is being prayed individually, an examination of conscience may be included. Here is a short examination of conscience; you may, of course, use your own method.

1. Place yourself in a quiet frame of mind.

2. Review your life since your last confession.

3. Reflect on the Ten Commandments and any sins against these commandments.

4. Reflect on the words of the Gospel, especially Jesus' commandment to love your neighbor as yourself.

5. Ask yourself these questions:
   Have I been unkind in thoughts, words, and actions?
   Am I refusing to forgive anyone?
   Do I despise any group or person?
   Am I a prisoner of fear, anxiety, worry, guilt, inferiority, or hatred of myself?

PENITENTIAL RITE (OPTIONAL)

If a group of people are praying in unison, a penitential rite from
the Roman Missal may be used:

All: I confess to almighty God
          and to you, my brothers and sisters,
          that I have greatly sinned,
          in my thoughts and in my words,
          in what I have done and in what I have failed to do,

And, striking their breast, they say:
          through my fault, through my fault,
          through my most grievous fault;

Then they continue:
          therefore I ask blessed Mary ever-Virgin,
          all the Angels and Saints,
          and you, my brothers and sisters,
          to pray for me to the Lord our God.

Presider: May almighty God have mercy on us,
          forgive us our sins,
          and bring us to everlasting life.

All: Amen.

HYMN: "BEHOLD A ROSE"

A hymn is now sung or recited. This traditional hymn was composed in German in the fifteenth century. It is sung to the melody of the familiar "Lo, How a Rose E're Blooming."

Behold, a rose of Judah
From tender branch has sprung,
From Jesse's lineage coming,
As men of old have sung.
It came a flower bright
Amid the cold of winter
When half spent was the night.

Isaiah has foretold it
In words of promise sure,
And Mary's arms enfold it,
A virgin meek and pure.
Through God's eternal will
She bore for men a savior
At midnight calm and still.

Psalm 40:2–8 Thanksgiving for Deliverance

Surely, I wait for the LORD;
    who bends down to me and hears my cry,
Draws me up from the pit of destruction,
    out of the muddy clay,
Sets my feet upon rock,
    steadies my steps,
And puts a new song in my mouth,
    a hymn to our God.
Many shall look on in fear,
    and they shall trust in the LORD.

Blessed the man who sets his security in the LORD,
    who turns not to the arrogant
    or to those who stray after falsehood.
You, yes you, O LORD, my God,
    have done many wondrous deeds!
And in your plans for us
    there is none to equal you.
Should I wish to declare or tell them,
    too many are they to recount.

Sacrifice and offering you do not want;
    you opened my ears.
Holocaust and sin-offering you do not request;
    so I said, "See; I come
    with an inscribed scroll written upon me.
I delight to do your will, my God;
    your law is in my inner being!"

RESPONSE

May all who seek after you be glad in the Lord,
may those who find your salvation say with continuous
praise, "Great is the Lord!"

SCRIPTURE READING

Read silently or have a presider proclaim the Scripture of the
day that is selected.

RESPONSE

Lord, you who were made obedient unto death, teach us to
always do the Father's will so that, sanctified by the holy
obedience that joins us to your sacrifice, we can count on
your immense love in times of sorrow.

Glory to the Father, and to the Son,
and to the Holy Spirit:
as it was in the beginning, is now,
and will be for ever. Amen.

SECOND READING

Read silently or have a presider read the words of
St. Augustine for the day selected.

CANTICLE OF SIMEON

Lord, now you let your servant go in peace;
  your word has been fulfilled:
my own eyes have seen the salvation
  which you have prepared in the sight of every people:
a light to reveal you to the nations
  and the glory of your people Israel.

Glory to the Father, and to the Son,
and to the Holy Spirit:
as it was in the beginning, is now,
and will be for ever. Amen.

PRAYER

Recite the prayer that follows the excerpt from
St. Augustine for the day selected.

BLESSING

Lord, give our bodies restful sleep and let the work
we have done today bear fruit in eternal life.
Watch over us as we rest in your peace. Amen.

MARIAN ANTIPHON

Hail, holy Queen, mother of mercy,
>   our life, our sweetness, and our hope.
To you do we cry,
>   poor banished children of Eve.
To you do we send up our sighs,
>   mourning and weeping in this vale of tears.
Turn then, most gracious advocate,
>   your eyes of mercy toward us,
>   and after this exile
>   show to us the blessed fruit of your womb, Jesus.
O clement, O loving,
O sweet Virgin Mary. Amen.

Sources and Acknowledgments

Augustine Day by Day II: Daily Readings From the Sermons of St. Augustine, compiled and edited by John E. Rotelle, OSA, Augustinian Press, 1995.

Letters of St. Augustine, edited by John Leinenweber, Triumph Books, Tarrytown, NY, 1992.

The Trinity by St. Augustine; introduction, translation and notes by Edmund Hill, OP; edited by John E. Rotelle, OSA; New City Press; Brooklyn, NY; Augustinian Heritage Institute; 1991.

Augustine of Hippo: Selected Writings (Classics of Western Spirituality series), translation and introduction by Mary T. Clark, Paulist Press, New York, 2002.

St. Augustine: Confessions, translation with an introduction and notes by Henry Chadwick, Oxford University Press, 1991.

The City of God by St. Augustine; translated by Marcus Dods, DD; introduction by Thomas Merton; the Modern Library; New York; copyright 1950 by Random House Inc.